THE CHANGES
WE MAKE FOR
LIFE

NANCY MARKISH

BALBOA.
PRESS
A DIVISION OF HAY HOUSE

Scripture quotations marked KJV are from the Holy Bible, King James Version (Authorized Version). First published in 1611. Quoted from the KJV Classic Reference Bible, Copyright © 1983 by The Zondervan Corporation.

Balboa Press books may be ordered through booksellers or by contacting:

Balboa Press
A Division of Hay House
1663 Liberty Drive
Bloomington, IN 47403
www.balboapress.com
1 (877) 407-4847

Because of the dynamic nature of the Internet, any web addresses or links contained in this book may have changed since publication and may no longer be valid. The views expressed in this work are solely those of the author and do not necessarily reflect the views of the publisher, and the publisher hereby disclaims any responsibility for them.

The author of this book does not dispense medical advice or prescribe the use of any technique as a form of treatment for physical, emotional, or medical problems without the advice of a physician, either directly or indirectly. The intent of the author is only to offer information of a general nature to help you in your quest for emotional and spiritual well-being. In the event you use any of the information in this book for yourself, which is your constitutional right, the author and the publisher assume no responsibility for your actions.

Any people depicted in stock imagery provided by Getty Images are models, and such images are being used for illustrative purposes only. Certain stock imagery © Getty Images.

Print information available on the last page.

ISBN: 978-1-9822-1882-9 (sc)
ISBN: 978-1-9822-1883-6 (e)

Balboa Press rev. date: 12/19/2018

Contents

Introduction

Our lives are the sum of our thoughts. What we think we are, we will be.

I used to hear the following statement regarding career perspectives: "Don't dress for the position you have, dress for the position you want". At first, I didn't see the point to this advice. It didn't make sense to "count your chickens before they hatch". But through the course of my life, and the changes I have made, I have learned that that is exactly what needs to be done. I came to understand that dressing for the position you want simply alters the way you view yourself, your goals, and what is possible. In changing your viewpoint (thoughts) you change the way you live your life.

When I started making serious life changes for myself, I didn't realize the full extent of what I was doing. Through counseling, reading, research and self-examination, I learned to make many changes in my life. But most often my focus started on the external part of my life, and therefore, I was taking the long, difficult way to accomplish my goal. What was actually making the changes was internal—the way I thought about myself with respect to the aspect of my life I needed to change.

When I learned where life changes really begin, future changes became easier. I learned to begin any change with my focus where it is more effective—in my thoughts.

It is my goal in this book to give you the information I learned in various types of life changes, the questions I learned to ask and the things I learned about changing the way I think, and how this knowledge helped me create a better life for myself.

CHAPTER 1
Who Do You Want To Be?

When we are young, we are often asked "WHAT do you want to be when you grow up?" We are encouraged to think about the career path we want to take and what our external interests are. But I have never heard anyone ask: "WHO do you want to be?" Before anyone can start making changes, they need to know why they want to make changes and what changes they need to make to accomplish their goals.

When we ask ourselves "Who do I want to be?", it is a question of what kind of person we want to be: kind, loving, mean, selfish, hard-working, fun-loving, spiritual, patient, materialistic, introvert, extrovert, and so on. There are many aspects and qualities to every individual. And we get to choose what we want to be. Just like we can choose a career for ourselves, we can choose the kind of person we want to be, and be that person. We can choose what qualities we admire in a person, what we would be proud to present to the world, and be that person. But first we need to have a very clear picture of who we want to be, to make the choices and decisions that will promote and form that person.

This may sound complicated, but it really isn't. It's just a matter of learning the habits and actions that will create what we want to be, and disallowing the habits and actions that will cause us to be what we do not want to be. For example, if we want to be a kind and patient person rather than an impatient rude person, it is a matter of choosing and learning the habits and actions of a kind and patient person. You will also disallow yourself to speak or act rudely.

If you have not taken the time to examine what kind of person you want to be, and what habits and boundaries you need to set in your life to be that person, you will allow yourself to be influenced by other people as to the actions and choices of conduct you make. This can be very harmful to your security as an individual and how you feel about yourself as a person. When we fail to define within ourselves what kind of person we are, and what kind of actions are suitable for our lives, we are subject to allowing ourselves to say and do things that we will not be proud of, actions we have been influenced by others to adopt. And this will undermine our sense of dignity, and cause us to be ashamed of the person we are presenting to the world.

On the other hand, if we have clearly defined to ourselves who we are, what kind of person we will be, and what actions and boundaries are allowed or disallowed in order to be that person, we will protect ourselves from outside influences. Who we are will not be subject to other people's opinions and actions, but will be governed by our own choices.

It is important to know what we want to be, how we want to live our physical lives. It is equally important to know who we want to be as a person. Knowing what kind of person we want to present to the world, and defining our boundaries and actions in order to be that person, will give us a healthy, self-assured foundation for all of what we do and accomplish in our lives.

Who do you want to be? And what will you do to make sure that is what you are?

CHAPTER 2
I Can Change If I Want To

Each day we are privileged to be able to choose how we live our lives. It may not seem like it, but each day we make decisions that decide the course of our lives, our happiness or unhappiness.

It's difficult to see how we are choosing our lives when things are not turning out like we want them to. This is a direct result of actions based on subconscious thoughts and decisions rather than conscious choices. We all have thought processes and habits that we are not aware of that effect our lives every day. And some of these thoughts and thought habits block us from changing the course of our lives and happiness. The belief systems we have, and the energies we create with these subconscious thoughts, take us in a different direction than what we desire to go.

The answer to change, in every aspect of our lives, is in changing our thoughts and thought processes, including our subconscious thoughts. And this is where we get stuck. We don't know how to change our thoughts.

To begin, we need to be able to identify what it is we are unhappy with and/or want to change in our life. This is where I use a form of meditation. When I am feeling a desire for change, I get myself in a quiet, meditative state and allow myself to "daydream" about the change I want to make. In our daydreams, we allow ourselves what our minds think is impossible and therefore get a clearer picture of what we want and why. Daydreams help us understand not only the physical aspect of what we want, but also the feeling associated with this change.

Once you know what it is you are wanting to change and what you want this change to be, you are then in a place to start examining what is blocking this change. It is now possible to identify the thought processes that have created choices that take you away from where you want to be.

We have been trained to believe that outside circumstances are the reason for not being able to accomplish that which we desire to do. However, the reality is that most outside circumstances can be changed by changing how one thinks and therefore acts or reacts regarding these circumstances. Change occurs in our perspectives first, and our actions second.

To begin the process of changing the thoughts that keep us from accomplishing our desires, we need to learn to hear our thoughts. I know this sounds silly, because if we think the thoughts we should be hearing the thoughts. But many of our thoughts and thought processes have become internal repetitive noise (habits). Just like any repetitive noise, we hear it on a subconscious level, but not in our conscious mind. We need to become consciously aware of the thoughts we have and how they affect our choices for our lives.

When you consciously examine your daydream, how you would want it to look and feel in reality, pay attention to your thoughts related to this dream. Do you hear yourself saying "that's impossible" or "I can't do that" or "I don't have the skills to accomplish that"? This is what you need to pay attention to. Challenge these thoughts. Ask yourself why it is impossible, ask yourself why you can't do that or what skills you think you lack. When you start becoming consciously aware of your thoughts and challenging the validity of these thoughts, you find that many of your beliefs (I can't do that) are thought habits that no longer are true in your life (or maybe never were). Some of the thoughts you will find were created from fear (and maybe still are), some of these thoughts were created from the opinions of other people, and so on. No matter where they came from, becoming aware of them is the first step in creating a mindset that will allow you to make your choices for your life in accordance to what you desire for your life.

I once was in a conversation with a friend and made the statement that I would have liked to have been a Broadway dancer. This friend asked me why I didn't do it. I blurted out, without conscious thought, "I didn't know I could". When I later examined this statement, I became aware that I, on a subconscious level, thought that, because I came from a small town and a poor family, becoming a Broadway dancer was beyond my reach. I look at that thinking today and realize how costly it was to my life experiences, and how utterly wrong it was. I realize today that there was a world of opportunity I could have used if I had allowed myself to be open to them; if I had challenged my own thoughts and beliefs. And this is a good example to me for the rest of my life. I learned to challenge the thoughts (and beliefs created by these thoughts) that prevent me from realizing my desires.

Challenging and replacing these self-defeating thoughts is the step that will begin to allow us to realize our desires. Every time we hear ourselves think a thought that is contrary to where we want to go or what we want to accomplish, stop. Challenge the validity of the thought. Is this thing possible? Is there more than one way to accomplish the same goal? Find new thoughts that will allow you to seek new answers and new choices. When your old thoughts say it is impossible, shut them down. Look at and think of the ways that it is possible. Allow your new thoughts to create new energies in your life.

When we become conscious and aware of the thoughts we are thinking and reacting to and actively work at replacing them with the thoughts that open our minds to new information and possibilities, we begin to create new energy in our lives. These new thoughts and energies will change the course of our lives. We can make our lives what we want them to be, but first we need to take control of our thoughts. We can choose how we live our lives by choosing what we think. And this is true of any area of our lives.

CHAPTER 3
Owning Our Lives

When we hear the term "ownership" it not only invokes the thought of possession, but of responsibility. When you own something, not only do you have the control over its use, but you have the responsibility for how it is used and how it is maintained.

Our lives are no different. Each one of us were given a life, we own it. With this ownership comes the responsibility of deciding how your life will be used and maintaining your life in a healthy manner, in order for it to function at its best.

This is a concept that's easy to comprehend on an outward, physical level. We need proper food, rest, and exercise to stay physically healthy. We need to maintain income and support to provide for our physical needs. We choose the way we care for and support our physical lives according to what we know about our own needs and happiness. But what about our internal needs? What care and maintenance are we giving to our soul, emotions and energies?

The effects of improper care and maintenance of your internal being is just as devastating to your person as improper physical care. Your internal person needs consistent checkups, nourishment, exercise and rest. We know that when we have not had the proper physical food and rest we are not able to concentrate and perform our day-to-day tasks as well as when we have had the needed rest and nourishment. We know that when we do not exercise as we should, our bodies become sluggish and weak. When we do not pay attention to changes in our bodies and have checkups to determine any needed changes to our care, we risk doing damage to our bodies. Our internal person, our souls, energies and emotions, are no different. To function as a healthy person, able to make healthy, productive choices, it requires the proper care of the inside of our being.

It's very easy to get caught up in the activity of our lives. Every day presents an endless list of things we need and want to do. One of those things that should be on that list is prayer and/or meditation. Through prayer and meditation, we are able to examine our energies, emotions and souls to determine if we have the nourishment, rest, and care we need. I'm sure we have all experienced feeling sad or dissatisfied with something in our lives, but not being able to identify the reason for this feeling. This is where prayer and meditation is effective. It allows us the time and focus to examine what is happening on the inside. Why our souls, energies and emotions are feeling need. When we are able to determine what the need is we are feeling, we are then able to seek solutions to fill this need.

This need can be as simple as rest. Perhaps you've been spending a great deal of time helping others and simply need some "me" time. Or maybe it goes deeper and your soul, energies and emotions are seeking a significant change in your life. Whatever the cause, making sure you provide time in your life for examining your internal life and providing what is needed will enable you to make clearer, more responsible decisions and choices. It will also help you to maintain your happiness by keeping your soul, energies and emotions healthy.

Another aspect of responsibility in owning your life is care and safety for yourself and others. How we make our choices, and the actions created by our choices, effects not only our lives but the lives of those around us. Carelessness, or not being fully aware due to lack of proper care, can cause hurtful, sometimes devastating effects, not only in our own lives, but also the lives of those we have interactions with throughout our days.

I think of this in a similar way to owning a car. A car is a wonderful tool in our lives. It provides us the freedom and ability to go places and seek opportunities we would not be able to do if we did not own this car.

However, without the proper maintenance, a car can become dangerous. When a car breaks down or stops working in the flow of traffic, it can cause an accident. The damage to property and even possibly someone's life will have an effect on everyone involved. Also, the improper use of a car: failing to obey traffic laws, drunk driving, tired driving, being distracted from your focus while driving; can produce the same results. It can cause damage to yourself and to the lives of those around you.

Operating your life, and your freewill, without proper care and maintenance, can be just as devastating to you and possibly those around you. If we live our lives each day without being aware of why we are making the choices we make, we risk making choices that are hurtful to our lives. If our internal life is needing care: rest, new direction, healing; and we do not take the time and care to provide these things, we risk making choices that may damage our lives and hurt those around us.

Sometimes we choose a drastic change to our lives, but only actually needed a little rest. If we had invested the time in doing a checkup on our internal life, we would probably have realized that we only needed to schedule some "me" time, and not change anything significant in our lives. Or maybe our internal being is wanting a change, or needing to heal an issue from the past. If we don't take the time to examine these feelings, identify the source, and know what it is we are wanting or needing, we could make a choice that will change our lives in unintended ways. And these choices may not only effect your own life, but also the lives of the people you interact with.

I love being able to choose my own life and direct my own happiness. It's wonderful. But it is at its best when I am making my choices from a state of health and proper maintenance. When I know that I have given my soul, energies and emotions the proper care, maintenance, time and attention, I can relax and enjoy the direction of my life, knowing that I am healthy and making sound, responsible choices. In our busy lives today, investing the time and energy to take proper care of your internal life will bring wonderful rewards in the form of good, responsible choices for you and those around you.

CHAPTER 4
Learning From the Past

The Past. It has already passed. It's done, over with. At least as far as what originally happened. But when we can't let it go, and replay these events over and over in our minds, it keeps the occurrence and the emotional result present.

Now this may not be a bad thing if what we are replaying in our minds is a positive, happy experience. Happy memories can bring a moment of joy and reaffirm the good things in life. However, living in the past more than we live in the present is harmful even with good memories.

If we spend too much of our thoughts and energies focused on the past, we are not living today, this moment. We are limiting our life experience to what has already happened, and not allowing ourselves to experience new joys. Even happy memories are most valuable when they are used to inspire new experiences, rather than reliving the past ones. If we allow our memories to inspire us to seek similar experiences again, we increase the value of the memory. It becomes a useful tool not only in reaffirming the goodness of these experiences, but also to inspire us to seek more of these same experiences. Just don't get stuck thinking about what used to be, but use this information to create what is today.

Negative, hurtful past experiences can be used to create more positive present experiences also. I know this may seem wrong when you first think about it. But think of it like a road map. If you are on a road trip that you have driven before, you know where you made any wrong turns, or what route you chose that took you where you wanted to be. Past experiences can be the same kind of useful tool. The positive memories will let us know what route took us where we wanted to be, the negative memories will tell us where we went wrong.

However, we probably won't comprehend where we made a wrong turn just because it happened. Sometimes we live similar negative experiences more than once because we failed to take the time and effort to examine what happened, why it happened and how to make different choices for a better outcome.

This may sound like I'm telling you to relive the past. Not so. When you allow your thoughts to replay an event in your life with no purpose other than thinking about what happened and how you felt/feel about it, that is simply reliving the past. However, when you allow yourself to think about these events with purpose and direction, intending to learn from these occurrences, you are now using the experience as a tool for future use. When you actively examine what happened, what your motivation was for making the original choice in this experience, and how you can change those choices for a more favorable outcome, you are now using the experience to create a better future.

The truly amazing thing about learning from the past to create a better future is that, in examining what happened, why we made the choice we made and using this information to direct our choices in the future, we often heal the wounds and pain from these experiences. Painful experiences, disappointments and tragic loss create wounds in our internal lives. Reliving painful and/or disappointing experiences and the pain involved, without direction or purpose, only keeps this wound open, sore and festering in our emotions, energies and thoughts.

(I have deliberately not included tragic loss in my last statement because tragic loss requires much more care and help than painful/disappointing experiences. If you have suffered tragic loss, I strongly recommend counseling and/or attending a group for people who have suffered similar loss.)

To turn a negative event in our lives into a positive, useful tool, we need to understand exactly what our real feelings about this event are. It's not enough to know you are hurt/angry/disappointed, etc. You need to know why you feel this way. When something happens that hurts us, we need to know what it is that makes it painful. Have you ever experienced being hurt by something someone said, but your friend who was also in the conversation was not hurt and does not understand why you were? It's the question of why that needs to be answered.

In looking at an event in your life (positive and negative), understanding why it is good or bad for you is the first step in using this event for your future. During my life, I have lived with several different roommates. Some of these experiences were positive and happy, some of these experiences turned out painful and disappointing. Overall, I would consider residing with a roommate in the future, if need be. Both the positive and the negative experiences have helped me know how to make a good decision in this regard. In examining the circumstances in each instance, I am able to understand what made me happy and why, and what hurt me and why. Knowing this information gives me clearer direction in making sound decisions in the future. I have the information to know what will work for me and what won't, and why.

This is the information that will help heal the wounds from negative experiences. Often, the most painful part of a negative experience is our feeling of vulnerability and powerlessness. When we continue to relive a negative past event, what we are truly trying to do is regain our sense of safety and power in our lives. However, just remembering the event and reliving the pain won't give that to you. You need to examine what choice you made and how that choice left you vulnerable and unprotected. Once you understand that, you will now have the information you need to not make that same choice in the future. When you know you are empowered to make a better choice, you begin to feel less vulnerable and more powerful in your life.

There are more aspects to healing wounds in our lives. But understanding your experiences, positive and negative, and how to use those experiences to create a better future for yourself is a great beginning. Reliving past without direction or purpose is a painful waste of our present energies, thoughts and emotions. Using the knowledge gained from examining and understanding the choices we made, and why or why not the result was a happy one, will empower us to create a better future. What has already happened cannot be changed. Understanding what happened, and using that information to make choices, can change what will happen in your future.

Don't get lost in the past. Don't let pain and disappointment ruin your future. Learn from your experiences and use them to create the world you dream of. Learn to use the knowledge you gained to empower your present and your future.

CHAPTER 5
Living in This World, Choosing Our Own Thoughts

I've talked about identifying the thoughts that are roadblocks to our happiness and changing those thoughts to produce new energies and results. This would be so much easier if we were insulated against the influences from the world around us. However, we cannot close ourselves away from the world, nor would we really want to. But taking control of our thoughts and thought processes means having to deal with the constant opinions, attitudes and teachings we are in contact with each day. This is where most of our roadblocks came from in the first place. So how do we keep from adding to the internal noise? If we are cleaning the internal noise out of our thoughts, how can we keep it from returning?

It is not possible to avoid hearing and mentally ingesting thoughts that can be roadblocks to our desires and goals. However, how we handle these thoughts when we encounter them will determine whether or not they stay in our thought processes and/or how much influence they will have on our own perspectives. This is another area where we need to practice actively listening.

Listen to the conversations we are involved in. Sometimes we may not even be an active part of the conversation, but if we are listening to one it will have an effect on us. Become aware of the words, tone and attitude behind these conversations. We can choose what we will allow our brains to accept and think about, and what we will reject. And we can do this on an immediate basis, so the internal roadblocks will not be allowed to function in our thought processes.

There are several methods I use to reject the thoughts that are contrary to the person I am and what I want my life to be. First, I disallow certain kinds of conversation in my life. I chose some time ago to be a kind, happy and positive person every day. To do this, I cannot think thoughts that are negative, unkind or angry. Therefore, I do not participate, either actively or inactively, in conversations that promote thoughts of unkindness, negative or aggressive attitudes, or lacking in gratitude. I simply refuse to allow my brain to participate in these thoughts. Being a human being, I sometimes slip up and some of the negativity gets in my brain. That's when I employ another method of keeping my thoughts clean.

When I catch myself thinking anything that is contrary to the person I am, or contrary to reaching my goals for my life, I simply employ the same method as I did for the internal noise I first started eliminating. I stop the thought, examine it, and replace unacceptable thoughts with positive, reaffirming thoughts. This may sound a little simplistic, but it does work. This method teaches our minds to reject that which is contrary to what we want to be. And we can learn to do this on an immediate basis, day to day, so that these roadblocks do not find a home in us.

The most difficult area of our lives to practice these methods is with family and friends. It's not intentional, it's their habits. Their internal noise/roadblocks will appear in their conversations and will be applied in the advice or concerns they express regarding your life. And it is difficult not to adopt the attitudes of those who are close to us. That's not to say we should not listen to the advice and concerns of others. Quite the contrary. It's through our conversations with trusted people that we often navigate through our own thoughts and feelings to discover our answers and solutions. However, when you examine any thought you acquired in these conversations, and that thought would work against who you are and what you want your life to be, reject it. Don't let it become a roadblock. Not every opinion or perspective is right for your life.

Employing these methods for keeping my thoughts in line with my desires and goals has enabled me to relax and enjoy the world around me to a greater degree. Because I know that I have developed the skills to maintain my life goals, and not let them be derailed by other people's thoughts and opinions, I am able to be less defensive in my interactions with others. I can allow them to express their perspectives and concerns without worry that they will influence me to not achieve my desires. I hear what they have to say, examine it to see if those thoughts work in my life goals, and decide whether to keep them or reject them.

Knowing that I am in control of my thoughts allows me the freedom to interact with the world in a more open manner. I can live in this world and still choose who and what I want to be.

CHAPTER 6
Happiness

Merriam-Webster Dictionary defines happiness in two ways: one definition is the state of being happy, the other is an experience that makes you happy.

We all love happy experiences, but our true desire is to live in a state of being happy. An overall contentment and satisfaction with our lives. To get an understanding of how to live in a state of happiness, we first need to understand that happy experiences happen; the state of being happy is a choice we make each moment of our lives.

What happened yesterday, how you felt about it and what you did to be happy or unhappy has no more effect on your life, other than the information you learned. You can look at the choices you made yesterday, and decide if they enhanced your happiness or not, and use that information to guide your choices for today. We also cannot make choices for tomorrow. We can dream, hope and plan, but the actual choices can only be made in the moment we live in. We choose to be happy (or not) at every moment of our day.

When we go about our day-to-day lives, a series of events will occur and how we choose to respond to these events will determine our overall happiness or lack of happiness. When positive things happen, the choice is easy. We just had a happy experience, it was a happy moment. The problem develops when we have painful, stressful, negative experiences.

How often do you feel frustrated in life because you feel happy and content, then down and sad? Does your happiness feel like it's attached to a yoyo? This is a very frustrating feeling. And one that can be changed.

We cannot prevent negative things from happening in our lives. It can range from as simple as someone being rude to us for no discernable reason to dealing with the deep pain and grief of the loss of a loved one. How we choose to view and respond to these moments in our lives will determine the stability of our happiness.

Most of the time we react to what happens to us and around us without much conscious thought. And this is fine, if your subconscious thoughts are directing you to make choices you are happy with. However, if you are having an issue with the stability of your happiness, examining the subconscious thoughts directing your choices is the first step you need to make. For example: did you wake up feeling happy and excited about your day, only to be in a bad mood by the time you got to work because someone cut you off in traffic and acted rudely to you? Did your subconscious thoughts direct you to feel defensive about your rights and angry because this person was disrespectful to you?

What would have happened if you replaced the self-defensive thoughts and anger with kindness and forgiveness? Perhaps this person had something happen this morning that distracted them in their driving. Maybe they didn't mean to be rude or disrespectful. Or even if they were being deliberately rude, what would happen if you choose to wonder what happened to them to make them so unhappy and gave them forgiveness anyway? Making a conscious choice to think and respond with happy thoughts rather than unhappy thoughts will change your feelings. It will also protect your happiness.

It doesn't matter what or who other people choose to be, or even what they think of you. What will create your happy life is the person you create within yourself and whether or not you are happy with that person.

The more we recognize negative, unhappy thoughts and the consequent actions, and consciously direct our thoughts and actions to support and promote our happiness, the more these positive, happy thoughts will become our subconscious thoughts. It will become natural for us to respond to the world around us in a positive manner, no matter what happens. These subconscious thoughts will protect and guide our overall happiness from moment to moment in our lives.

But what about the tragic losses and pain in life? The death of a loved one, the loss of a limb or your health, the loss of your job, etc.? This kind of pain requires much more attention and healing. Tragic loss causes a wound in our souls. And just like physical wounds, these internal wounds need to heal in a proper manner to be able to return to a healthy function in life.

Most of our lives function according to set patterns we have chosen for ourselves. Our education, marriage, children, careers, hobbies, etc. We approach each day making our choices according to our concept of our lives and the happiness we pursue. When we suffer a tragic loss, it alters the concept of our life. And this is what creates the wound. There is at least a portion of our lives we can no longer view the way we used to. This will alter the state of our overall happiness for a time. But if we have chosen to seek proper healing, our thoughts and choices will return us to a state of contentment and happiness. Just as when we receive a physical wound, an internal wound will alter our normal functions until healing is complete. However, just as with a physical wound, the more we heal and the stronger we become, the more we are able to return to making the choices that will produce the happiness we desire.

Another area of life that plays havoc with our happiness is not yet having realized our hopes and dreams the way we desire them. As stated previously, we have the freewill and the ability to make our own choices for our lives, whether we will pursue a certain course or not. And we may be in the process of seeking the information and changing our thought processes so we can realize these dreams. But getting to where we want to be can be a long journey. It can be difficult to hold onto our faith and commitment to our dreams. How we handle the struggle with faith and commitment to our dreams and goals can affect the stability of our happiness.

The realization of dreams and hopes can only affect the stability of your happiness if you have chosen to think of your happiness as dependent on the achievement of your goal. In other words, if you think that you cannot be happy until and unless you achieve your goal, you have reduced your state of happiness to a singular experience. In this point of view, you will always have fluctuating happiness, dependent on the occurrence of happy experiences. The state of being happy is a choice to be happy at this moment, with what is. When you can view the achievement of your goals and dreams not as your complete happiness but as another aspect of your happiness, you can maintain the stability of your happiness while working to add to it. If, in the future, you decide to abandon this dream, you will not be abandoning your happiness, but just a certain aspect of it. Your overall state of happiness will remain intact.

Happiness—the state of being happy—is a choice. You can choose to relinquish your happiness to the negativity in the world around you and to your old thought habits; or you can choose to exercise your freewill to direct your thoughts, thought habits, and the consequent actions created by them, to achieve a consistent state of happiness. This is not always an easy thing to accomplish. It takes work to pay attention to your mind and the choices you are making. But if your happiness is important, it's worth the work. Happiness will not happen to you. Happiness is a choice you make every moment of your life.

CHAPTER 7
Know Yourself—Save Your Relationships

There are extremely few people in this world who would enjoy a life of complete solitude. Most of us crave relationships and interaction with other people. We're supposed to. However, interactions between human beings is a complicated minefield of opportunity for conflict.

It is sometimes difficult to find those people that have similar viewpoints to our own. And even when we do, there are still areas of differences. We fight more with the ones we have the closest relationships with, because the closeness allows more opportunity for differences to surface and conflict to take place. Unfortunately, all too often, these conflicts result in damage to and/or the loss of the relationship. Once we have suffered this damage or loss, we then spend a considerable amount of time, focus and energy to repair our feelings and hopefully our relationship. How much better would it be if these conflicts could be prevented in the first place? It isn't realistic to think we can prevent all conflict. However, it is possible to minimize the amount of conflict we have, and minimize the damage that is done in the conflict we cannot avoid.

Have you ever had a fight with someone and, in replaying the event in your mind, you realize that you had failed to tell the other person something, or were angry because you thought they knew something that they didn't actually know? Unfortunately, by the time you realize that you were holding the other person accountable for something they did not know, you have hurt them, yourself, and caused damage to the relationship.

There are times in my life when I have looked back on a lost relationship, or a fight I had with a loved one, and realized that I didn't say some of the things I should have said. I realized that there were things I wanted them to understand, but failed to tell them. This usually happens because in looking back and replaying the conflict, I came to a realization about my own feelings and needs that I didn't previously understand. Since I didn't understand these things about myself, I was not able to help my loved one understand.

Professional counselors address this issue when helping people resolve conflicts. They ask questions such as: What were your feelings at the time? Why did you feel this way? What could help you to feel differently? By asking these questions it helps individuals become more aware of their own feelings and needs so that they can communicate them to their loved one. The answers to such questions will help the other person understand your needs and point of view. But what is not often acknowledged is that many times the person answering the questions is just then becoming aware of the information also. It wasn't just a matter of failing to communicate the information. It was a matter of not realizing that these needs and wants existed in the first place.

To prevent or minimize the damage in conflict it is necessary to practice preventative maintenance in our lives. Just as we eat healthy, get enough rest and exercise to minimize the chance for becoming sick, or practice safety measures to minimize our chance of being injured, so can we practice preventative measures to minimize the chances of conflict in our relationships and the resulting damage. The more you know about yourself, your needs, wants, and boundaries, the more you can minimize conflict and the resulting damage.

Even in long standing relationships, there are times when misunderstandings happen. That's because life is ever changing. And we naturally adjust and change with it. But sometimes we are not aware of our true feelings about the changes taking place, or what we need and want in these changes. Because we have not taken the time and energy to be fully aware of the changes taking place and what it means for our lives, how we really feel, what we really want, we act and react on inadequate knowledge and misinformation. This in turn causes us to give misinformation, or inadequate information, to the people we are in relationships with.

What is really needed here is a conscious effort to stay in tune with your life. Just like you take the time to eat properly, get enough rest and exercise and practice safety measures, so should you invest the time and energy to stay in tune with your internal needs throughout the changes taking place in your life.

This doesn't require a pilgrimage to a holy place to experience self-enlightenment. It is simply being aware of changes occurring in your life and taking the time and focus to examine these changes and your reactions to them and making sure that you are making your choices based on the knowledge you have of your true needs and wants. Knowing how you really feel, and making sure you can communicate these feelings, will greatly reduce the conflicts and/or damage from conflicts in your life.

Many times, conflicts are a direct result of each person not being aware of their own true feelings and, because of not knowing, making assumptions about what the other person needs or wants. This is dangerous ground. It's like trying to avoid landmines in the dark. And very unnecessary.

Take the time to make sure you know what it is you need and want at each turn in your life. And when these turns include people you are in a relationship with, you'll be able to help them understand what choices you need to make and why. The more we understand about ourselves and each other, the easier it is to work through the changes without causing unnecessary damage to ourselves and our relationships.

Even when we are caught up in a moment of anger and conflict, we need to take a step back for a minute, examine the issue of the conflict and what we truly feel about it. Not just about being mad or feeling we are being treated unfairly, but why we feel this way, what it is we need, what solution we are looking for. We are then able to come back to the issue with more knowledge and more equipped to work through to a solution.

There is an added benefit to learning to be aware of our needs and wants and being able to communicate these things to the people we are in relationships with. That benefit is that we will also be able to know how to make sure we are understanding the person we are in a relationship with, their needs and wants. When we know what we want and need, and know what the other person wants and needs, it becomes much more possible to find resolution and minimize damage to our relationships.

Before you react to your anger and frustration, take a moment to make sure you are not making an untrue assumption that the other person does not care about your feelings, needs and wants. Make sure you are fully aware of what you need and want, why you need and want it and that you have given this information to the other person. Also, take the time to make sure you understand what it is the other person needs and wants. The effort and energy you spend in doing so will be rewarded in the form of better relationships.

Just as you spend time and energy to take care of your body, invest the time and energy to take care of your relationships. Before you make a choice, by word or deed, that may damage your relationship, make sure you truly know what it is you want and need. Make sure that you have given this information to the other person.

For me, I'd rather spend the time, energy and focus preventing damage than try to repair the damage after it is done. The effort it takes to be able to minimize conflict is rewarded by not having caused hurt to myself and my loved ones.

CHAPTER 8
What You Don't Know Can Hurt You

Today I was thinking about a few times in my life when I needed an answer from God, some direction regarding a decision I needed to make in my life, and felt stuck. I prayed, but just couldn't seem to hear the answer. It felt like God was not answering my prayer, not giving me any direction or help. Until the day came that I could not wait any longer. I had to have an answer. I needed to hear from God. And I got very serious.

I was so desperate for an answer that I stopped what I was doing, put everything else on hold, and just focused on talking to God and seeking to hear his answer. I took the time and energy to concentrate on this one issue. And when I did, it did not take very long to get an answer.

As I was reflecting on these times, I realized that it never was a matter of God not trying to answer my prayer and give me the direction I sought. It was a matter of my inability to understand what God was trying to tell me. I was so focused on the issue at hand, and trying to figure out what decision to make, that I was not open to new information. God needed me to get in a quiet, focused place so He could teach me something new, and consequently open up my ability to accept other options than what I thought was possible.

Looking back on these times, I realized that when I am in a situation where I can't seem to get an answer from God, I need to ask God to help me to allow Him to show me, and help me understand, the answer I cannot comprehend. Sometimes to answer our prayers in the best manner, God needs to teach us other options than the ones we are aware of. God will help us make decisions and choices, but will not force us to choose any particular one. So, if there is an option we are not aware of, we will not be able to choose that option. When God knows that the best answer to our prayers is an option we are unaware of, we need to be able to allow God to make us aware of this option.

God reminded me today that when I cannot seem to find the answer to a situation in my life, I need to change my focus from making a decision, to allowing God to show me choices I am not aware of. The feeling of being "stuck" regarding a decision in my life is a clear indicator that there is something I need to learn. When I have taken the time to focus on what God is trying to teach me, rather than knowing what decision to make, I have always gained the knowledge that led me to a better choice than I thought was possible.

It is not only important to allow ourselves to hear God's direction in our lives, but it is also important to learn to allow God to show us the information and options that are beyond what we think is possible in our lives. Feeling "stuck" about making a decision is not a dead end. It is an opportunity to learn about the choices and options that are available to us beyond what we know or can see. It is an opportunity to avail ourselves of God's infinite knowledge and wisdom.

The more we know about our options in life, the better choices and decisions we can make for ourselves. But we don't always know that there is more information to be had. We don't know that we have other options than the ones we are aware of. This is where God will answer our prayers in the most perfect manner. Because God will give us the information we lack so we can make the best choice. We just need to be willing to listen and learn.

The next time you find yourself having a difficult time making a choice in an important matter, and feeling like you cannot hear God's answer, take the time to meditate and focus on allowing yourself to learn what it is God is trying to show you. You may very well become aware of a better choice than you previously knew was possible.

CHAPTER 9
Stop Whining - So You Can Hear God

Picture this scenario: a child wants a horse and asks his/her parents for one. The parents tell the child no, not now. They say this because they plan to enroll their child in riding lessons before purchasing the horse. The lessons will help the child be prepared to ride the horse when they get it. The child throws a fit, whining and crying because, in their perspective, his/her parents are being unloving and not caring about what the child wants/needs. The parents may try to explain to the child that they plan to enroll them in riding lessons in preparation for owning a horse in the future, but the child can't hear them because of their whining and crying. When the child finally calms down, he/she may be able to listen and know that their desires are known, and that his/her parents are preparing them to receive their desires in the future. But if the child stays angry, whining and not listening, the child will not know that there is no reason for their disappointment, other than their own perspective and lack of knowledge. The child is preventing themselves from receiving what they want, by not listening to what is needed to get it.

This is the same scenario we go through with God. We pray and ask God to provide things for us. Careers, money, relationships, material possessions, and so on. When we ask God for these things, often we see the answer to our prayers as being immediate. We want a "yes" answer all the time, without delay. But God knows that to give us our best answer, sometimes it takes some preparation. Sometimes we are not ready for the thing we are praying for.

This is not a "no" answer, but a "not now" answer. God does not give us a "not now" answer because He's too busy. A "not now" answer means that there is some preparation that needs to be made to be able to receive what we are asking for. As in the case of the child wanting the horse, it wouldn't do them much good to have one if they didn't know how to ride it, nor would it be safe for them. And so it is with many things we pray for. Sometimes we are not prepared to receive what we are asking for. And God tells us "not now".

Even being adults, we often are not much different than the child in the example. When we pray for something, and it seems like our prayers are not being answered, we start questioning if God is hearing us, answering us, caring for what we need and want. We start feeling sorry for ourselves because we are disappointed not to have received what we want, when we wanted it. But this is the time we need to stop whining and throwing a fit, and ask God to show us what we need to learn to realize our dreams and goals.

The child in the example would have saved him/herself upset and grief if he/she had simply asked the parents why they could not have the horse now. Hearing the answer: 'because you need riding lessons first" would have helped the child know that they would be getting a horse in the future. It would also have given the child the incentive to learn what was needed so he/she would be prepared to get the horse.

It is no different with us and God's answers to our prayers. Often, the fact that we have not achieved a goal or desire is because of something we do not know or understand. We lack the knowledge and ability to achieve what we are praying for. This is not the time to throw a fit and doubt God. This is when we need to open ourselves to God's direction, and allow Him to lead us to the knowledge and lessons that will help us achieve our goals.

When you are wondering why a prayer does not seem to be answered, or think that God does not care about what you want and need, instead of whining, feeling disappointed and uncared for, open your mind and soul to God and listen to what He's trying to tell you. Ask God to help you understand what you need to learn to achieve your dreams, goals and desires. You will save yourself time and unnecessary grief if you stop whining and start listening. Trust God not only to give you your needs and desires, but to make sure that you are prepared to enjoy them to their fullest.

CHAPTER 10
God's Awesome Love

Recently I took a flight that departed the airport after dark. As the plane was ascending, I looked out over the landscape, admiring the look of the city at night. The lights, the movement, the neighborhoods and commercial districts. I started picturing just one person moving about in all that space, cars, buildings and other people. I couldn't help thinking about how small the life of any one individual really is. I couldn't help thinking about my life. How small I am compared to the vastness of our planet. How seemingly insignificant I am compared to the vastness of the number of people in our world. Just one person compared to all that exists in our world. And then the most amazing thought crossed my mind. God knows I exist, loves me and cares about my life.

This may not seem like an amazing thought. But when I looked out that plane window, and considered all the people living in just the space I could see, it seems almost impossible that God would know that I am even alive, much less who I am and what my life is about. And yet, I know He does. There have been too many miracles, blessings and answered prayers for me to deny that God knows who I am, hears my prayers, and blesses me with his love and care. And I am humbled by the enormity of such a gift.

It is beyond my ability to truly grasp the magnitude of the world we live in. As I looked out that plane window, my mind tried to picture all the people in just the city I could see, and what was happening in all their lives. All the issues, problems and needs of the people in just one city. Food, clothing, shelter, marriage issues, family problems, job problems, drugs and alcohol issues, health problems, career choices, hate crimes, violence, grief, disappointments, and on and on. All these issues for so many people. And my mind couldn't comprehend it. Not even for just one small city, much less the entire planet.

And then I couldn't help considering my own arrogance. I, like most other people, go about my day in a state of total self-importance. It's not that any of our lives are unimportant, but I tend to forget just how relatively insignificant most of the things I consider important really are. When I looked out the plane window, and thought about all the people and all the needs in this one small corner of the world, I couldn't help but marvel at God's patience and love for me.

Despite my arrogant, self-important viewpoint, and the relative insignificance of my needs and wants, God still hears my prayers, cares about my life and blesses me. And that is so awesome! In truth, my mind is incapable of truly comprehending that kind of love. In all of my life, and all of my prayers to God, God has never once allowed me to feel that my prayers, needs, wants or desires were less important to Him than anyone else's. And that kind of love is far above my understanding.

I'm glad I looked out that plane window that night. I may not be able to comprehend all I could see, and all that encompasses our world, but I am grateful for the bigger picture. I am grateful for the opportunity to have a greater understanding of the vastness and awesomeness of God's love for me. It is greater than I can ever truly understand.

CHAPTER 11
A Still, Small Voice

Listen, shshshsh

Listen, do you hear it? Hear what? You might ask. That still, small voice. Have you ever experienced a quiet "thought" that was completely new to you and yet inspired you? Or been in despair, but all of a sudden had a reminder of a comforting verse or statement?

Most of us believe that God speaks to us in a still, small voice. But do you know why? Why not just speak to us in a regular voice? Or better yet, why not speak to us in a sonorous or booming voice, like is depicted in the movies? I think if God spoke to us in a deep, booming voice we'd definitely know it was him. On the other hand, it might scare us to death. A loud noise will get our attention, but so will a whisper.

So why the still, small voice? I asked God about this one day. He started his explanation with a memory of an incident that happened when I was a teenager still residing in my parent's home.

One of my older sisters was married and she and her husband were visiting at my parent's home for the weekend. On Saturday evening, the kitchen was crowded with me, my parents, a couple of my siblings and my brother-in-law. Now, we're a large and very talkative family, so the din in the kitchen was considerable and considerably loud. All of a sudden, the whole kitchen got quiet. And we were all looking around to find out why.

We lived in an old farmhouse that had the floor/ceiling vents that allowed heat from the downstairs to travel upstairs. One such vent was in the kitchen venting heat to the bathroom directly above. My sister had been upstairs taking a bath while the group in the kitchen was talking and being loud. She needed her husband to get something for her. What caused us to get quiet was the fact that she whispered through the vent to my brother-in-law.

Now, logic would say that my brother-in-law should not have been able to hear her over the noise of our conversations in the kitchen. But he did. And so did the rest of us. As a matter-of-fact, he asked her why she was whispering and she told him that she had tried to call to him several times, but could not get his attention. So she tried whispering, and got not only his immediate attention, but the rest of ours also.

I've thought about this event several times in my life. I usually thought of it as relating to our penchant for being "in on" secrets. I always figured that the reason we all got quiet was because we thought there was a secret about to be told and wanted to know. And that may have been part of it.

But when I asked God about speaking in a still, small voice, he showed me this incident and another perspective about it. By whispering, she input a sound into the din that was not easily recognized by my brother-in-law's ears or brain. He had to stop and pay attention to what he was hearing, in order to know what the sound was. She got his attention. What God showed me about the incident with my sister and her husband was that it wasn't so much about a possible secret, but it was a completely different sound than all the other noises we were hearing. We had to focus to hear her voice and what she was saying.

Our day-to-day lives are rather noisy. Not only to the ear, but also internally. We have so many voices to be heard. Sometimes our lives are so crowded with things to be done, needs to be met and conversations to be had, that we have trouble hearing our own voices. Can you imagine God trying to get a word in edgewise? But he does, because he knows how. He speaks to us in a still, small voice. God knows how to get our attention. We can be going through our noisy days, scrambling to hear our own thoughts, but when God speaks in a still, small voice, we will notice. We will know that there is a sound that is not part of the daily din of life. We will recognize that we heard something that needs our attention.

When our ears hear a noise, speech, etc. that is loud, our brains are able to pick up this information without much effort. However, when we notice something is spoken softly, it causes our brains to stop whatever else we were thinking about and focus on retrieving the quiet information. If we hear a faint noise that we cannot identify, we will automatically be quiet and focus on that noise so that we can identify it and decide if it needs our further attention. Softly spoken words do the same thing. When someone speaks quietly to us, or around us, we will quiet the noise in our minds, and sometimes around us, so we can hear what is being said. This also causes our minds to focus more sharply on the words being said and the information being given.

When we have quieted all the other noise, our brains cease to process that information. This leaves more mental "space" for processing what we are focusing on. And therefore, we are comprehending more precisely and retaining this information better. We are more aware of what is being said and what the meaning of this information is. Our minds are being given the space to process it. And this is where listening becomes so very important. How often do you think we miss what God is trying to tell us on any given day? We hear that quiet voice, but we don't take the time and focus to listen. Sometimes we feel like God is not listening to our prayers and our needs, but the truth is, we are not listening to God's answers. We have not taken the time and focus to listen to what his still, small voice is trying to tell us.

And taking the time to listen to what God has said is another reason he speaks in a still small voice. When someone or something is very loud, we don't have much choice but to acknowledge the information. Loud voices and loud noises command attention from us. But God gave us a freewill, and this includes listening to him. God does not want to command us to listen to him. He wants us to listen because we choose to. So, when he speaks to us in a still, small voice, it allows us the choice to listen or ignore him. We can choose to hear his words, focus on his voice and receive the information he is offering us, or we can choose to allow our daily lives and the noise therein to drown out his voice and ignore his direction and assistance. Unfortunately, this has become a habit that is all too common among us. We have allowed our lives, and the day to day events in our lives, to become more important than the direction of God. So even when we hear his voice, we turn from it and ignore the answers we have been asking for. And God won't make you listen, but that won't mean he didn't try to give you the answer you asked for.

How important is God's help, God's answers in your life? Is it worth taking the time to really listen and understand the direction he's trying to give you? Next time you hear that still, small voice, and you will hear it: Stop. Pay attention. Know that God is trying to get you to choose to give his words and direction attention and focus. After all, you asked him for his help and he's trying to give it to you. But he won't force it on you with a loud, commanding voice. He will offer your answers to you in a still, small voice.

CHAPTER 12
Life is a Partnership With God

When we are in business with a partner, that business functions at its best when each partner knows what skills and knowledge they are bringing to the project, what part of the business is their responsibility and is under their governance, what part of the business belongs to the expertise and governance of their partner, and respecting the balance. Usually a partnership is formed to bring the skills and expertise of more than one person to a project or endeavor. By allowing each person to use their special skills and knowledge in this endeavor, the outcome will produce better results than one person trying to supply every aspect of this project, some of which will be out of their abilities and knowledge.

Our lives were created to be a partnership with God. There are the parts that have been given to us to govern (our freewill), and those parts that are meant for God to govern (God's will). Having a healthy, balanced life depends on knowing and respecting this balance. A productive life depends on maintaining your part of the partnership and allowing God's part of the partnership to properly function in your life.

I have often said in my life that many small businesses fail because the person starting the business does not get help with the management side of the business. Maybe you're an excellent carpenter and attempt to go into business for yourself. You know how to build quality products, you have a good reputation for providing good workmanship at a fair price, and you have a good customer base. But your business fails to survive and/or thrive and you don't know why.

Often, this is a case of not having utilized the expertise of someone who knows how to make a business function properly and manage the financial side of it. Creating a product or service that will be purchased by the public is one thing, knowing how to handle the financial flow, marketing, customer service and all other aspects of the business is the other part. Creating a successful business depends not only on creating a marketable product/service, but also being able to manage the functions of the business in a productive manner.

It is possible to obtain the necessary knowledge to be able to fulfill all functions of a business on your own. A carpenter can learn to manage the financial flow, the marketing of the service/product and handle the customer service. But at what cost? The time and energy that would be consumed learning the necessary skills and performing these functions will greatly reduce the time and energy spent producing the product/service. When we are creating the thing we have to give to this world, our area of expertise, utilizing the skills of a partner that will help us succeed and thrive will greatly accelerate our ability to reach our goals.

Our lives are no different. When we attempt to use our own power, skills, and knowledge without assistance and direction from God, it is like trying to succeed in a business based solely on our ability to create a product or service, and what we do or do not know about how to manage the business. Success will be limited to our own capabilities and knowledge. So how does one have a partnership with God?

At times in my life I have been caught in sort of a seesaw of trying to respect and submit to God's will, but also use the freewill God gave me. It has been a very confusing subject, because I just couldn't figure out when or how to submit to God's will and when and how to use my will. It finally occurred to me to ask God this question: If we, as humans, are supposed to do Your will, why would you give us a freewill of our own?

That was the open-door invitation God was waiting for from me. My openness to understand the relationship God has been trying to build with me. A partnership in my life. If you look at your life as your product or service to this world, God is the partner with the skills to make your business a success. What's required on your part is to know who you are and what you want to give to this world in your life. Once you know that, you need to build a relationship with your partner (God). To build this partnership, you will need to know what areas are your expertise and domain, what areas are God's expertise and domain, and build a respectful, balanced partnership based on this knowledge.

Your area of expertise/domain: these are the things we desire to do, experience and accomplish in our lives. Each one of us impacts the world around us no matter how simply we think we live. Maybe you are someone who dreams of making a major scientific breakthrough that will impact the entire world. Or maybe you are a person who wants to live a quiet life raising a family in a small town, being a teacher or working for a local company. Either way you are impacting the world. This choice, the life you choose, is your product/service to the world. This is what you get to choose and govern: what that life will be.

God's area of expertise/domain: God is the knowledge bank. God knows what skills, opportunities and resources you will need to accomplish your life business. God knows where and how to find these things and will provide the knowledge needed for you to do what you desire to do. God is also the power and energy behind the opportunities we receive. Have you ever experienced this in your life: you find yourself at the right place, at the right time, to receive something you were hoping for? But when you think about what caused you to be there you are amazed, because you weren't going to go there, but something caused you to want to go at the last minute? Or maybe it was a time when you were just going about your business as usual, but something out of the ordinary happened that created an opportunity for you to receive that which you were needing. This is God fulfilling his part of the partnership. Providing the knowledge, opportunities and energies to help you accomplish your desires and goals in life.

The partnership balance: knowing and respecting the domain of each partner. You have to understand and take responsibility for knowing who you are as a person, what you want to do with your life (your life business) and how you want to do what you have chosen to do with your life. If you are lazy about examining your desires and goals and consciously making a plan in your life, God will not overstep his domain. God cannot become your business partner if you have not established a business. God will help you determine what it is you desire to do by providing the opportunities for knowledge and insights to your desires. But you ultimately must make the choice. That is not as scary as it sounds. Because God will also help direct our paths. We don't have to worry about a "wrong" choice because God will fulfill his part of the partnership by providing knowledge and direction. If we make a choice that is contrary to what we were wanting to accomplish, God will help direct us back to the proper path. Our domain is to take responsibility for choosing our direction in life and pursuing those goals.

Respecting God's domain means hearing, listening and acting upon God's direction. It never does any good to have a business partner if you consistently ignore your partner's advice, overstep your partner's area of expertise/domain, and fail to allow your partner's knowledge and skills to promote your business. If you refuse to allow your partner to be a partner, then you may as well just go it alone. If you want God to be your partner in life, you must make every effort to respect God's direction and assistance. This starts with listening. If you refuse to pay attention to what God is trying to tell you, it is completely your own responsibility for not knowing the information. God will send you the information you need to succeed, but you must be willing to hear it and learn it. We also must be willing to act upon God's direction.

Acting upon God's direction can be a little confusing. Sometimes it is difficult to know whether God is trying to guide us in a certain direction, or whether it is our own thoughts and desires directing our decision. What we need here is trust. Just as we trust a business partner to help us fix things if we make a wrong decision in business, so can we trust God to help us if we make a "wrong" choice in life.

I have made many "wrong" choices in my life. I put the word wrong in quotation marks because it may not have been the correct path I was aiming for, but oftentimes was not technically wrong because the choice enabled me to learn important information for my life. Sometimes I have had to take a little detour to correctly understand the direction and information God was leading me to. And sometimes when I thought a choice was the right one, but was not, God just simply lead me back to where I needed to be. It's ok. That's why God is our partner. If we knew how to do everything ourselves, and had all the right answers, we wouldn't need God as a partner. But when we actively strive to listen to God's direction and act upon it, God will help us succeed in our goals and desires.

The desires and goals we have in our lives is a direct reflection of the person we were created to be. God gave us a freewill so that we can pursue the paths in life that reflect the person we were created to be. God's will for us is to supply the support and partnership we need to succeed in being the person we were created to be. God's will is to use his power and knowledge to give us every assistance we need to be that which we are meant to be. If you use your freewill to not only choose your path in life, but to allow God to be your partner, you will find your success and fulfillment in life much, much easier to obtain.

CHAPTER 13
Submitting Our Will To God's Will

When we say the word submission without any context, it brings to mind someone whose will has been broken, who is now subservient to another through force and coercion. But this is rarely the case. Most of the time we practice submission without even realizing it. We submit our own will to that of the governmental law, to social conformity, and many other ways that we allow ourselves to be governed by the will of others.

So why is the idea of submitting ourselves to God such a seemingly difficult thing to do? It's a matter of trust. Trusting that God will not ask for our submission to his will without regard to our happiness.

Being able to willingly submit to another's will is very much dependent on knowing and trusting that our security and happiness will be protected. We submit to governmental laws because we believe that they are made for our protection and security. We submit to social conforms because we believe they are rules and guidelines for our social happiness and security. God will never force us to submit to his will. God asks us to submit to his will, knowing that we will need to trust Him to care for our security and happiness.

So why should we trust God and submit to His will? Because He sees the big picture. Humans have shown time and again our capability to learn and create things. We have shown many times, even as individuals, our abilities to accomplish great things. But we have also shown our finite knowledge by the problems and mistakes we have made. How often has man created things, or chosen solutions to problems, that later proved to cause additional problems in our lives? Would trusting God, and allowing his greater knowledge to guide us, eliminate the problems caused by our lack of seeing the big picture?

When I consider this question, I often think of raising my children. How often would my sons have saved themselves some grief if they had listened to what I tried to tell them? I had their best interests in mind, and because I had lived and experienced things they had not, I had information they did not have. I don't think their choice not to listen to me was based in distrust of my care for them. I believe they just didn't think I understood what they thought would make them happy. They distrusted my ability to know them as a person, and to help them find solutions according to their own needs and desires.

I believe it is the same for us to submit our will to God's will. It's not a matter of believing that God loves us and wants what is best for us. Most of us do believe that. But it is a matter of believing that God knows us as an individual: our hopes, dreams, desires, insecurities, pain and suffering and feelings. To truly submit our will to God's will, we need to truly believe that God knows us as an individual. That God's will and guidance includes our needs and desires as well as His needs and desires.

It is easy to trust another person to make a choice for us, if we trust them to know what we need and what will make us happy, and that they will choose accordingly. When we know we have communicated our feelings to this person, and they have shown us that they understand and will care for our needs and desires, it is easy for us to trust them. Our difficulty in trusting God to consider our personal feelings, needs and desires comes from our lack of communication with God. We fail to talk to God about the specifics of our needs and dreams.

Talking to God about the specifics of our needs and dreams is what will help create our trust that He will consider us as an individual when exercising His will. Yes, we believe that God knows us better than we know ourselves. But when we talk to God about our personal wants and needs, we are reassuring ourselves that God knows how we feel, what we want, who we are as a person. This is not for God's sake, but for our own. As imperfect humans, we need the physical expression to God to assure ourselves that he knows. The more specifically we talk to God about our needs and desires, the more trust we are able to exercise in God's will in our lives. The more trust we have in God to include our happiness in his will, the more willingly we will submit to His will. And submitting our will to God, knowing that He will offer a more complete and successful solution to our needs and desires, will bring us the happiness and security we seek.

Submitting to God's will is not something we have to do. God will never force or coerce us to submit to him. Our submission is something God wants us to give of our own free will. Willingly submitting our will to God will allow God to offer us choices and direction beyond our own capabilities. Learning to talk to God about who we are as a person: our likes and dislikes, our hopes and dreams, fears and insecurities, will give us the surety that God knows who we are and what we want as an individual. Feeling secure that God knows you as an individual, and will care for your individual needs and desires in exercising His will, allows you to willingly submit your will to His.

When you find yourself trying to give your cares and dreams to God, but struggling to trust God's will, take the time to talk to God about what it is you are afraid He won't know, or care for, when you submit to His will. Talk to God about who you are, what you dream of, what you worry about, what you need. Talk to God about who you are as a person. When you do, you will know that he knows you, and you will be able to more readily trust His will to include your needs and desires. You will be able to submit to God's will because you will trust Him to know the person you are and care for your happiness and security.

CHAPTER 14
Worry

Speaking for myself, I hate to be worried. Worried about what might or might not happen. Worried about something not turning out the way I think it needs to. Worried about not being able to pay a bill or accomplish a task. Worried about so many things in life. It's exhausting and robs me of enjoying everything else. It also is a useless waste of my energies.

When I think of worry and what it does for me, it's all negative. I cannot think of anything positive that worry accomplishes. Worrying does not solve any problems, real or imagined. Worry does not stop bad things from happening. Worry does not produce more money or resources. So, what does worry do?

Worry drains our energy and prevents us from seeing and experiencing the joy and happiness of our lives. Worry is the action of allowing fear to continually return our attention to trying to solve a problem that we do not have the power or knowledge to solve. It is a useless activity. If we can prevent something from happening, we would know this and would take the steps to do so. If we think we can prevent a problem, but do not know how, worrying will not give us that information. Research and learning will give us that information. If we fear that we will make the wrong decision, worrying will not make us feel more secure about our choice.

So how do we stop wasting our time and energy on worry? By accepting the fact that we cannot control everything that will happen in our lives. By learning to allow God's will and assistance into our lives. By submitting our wills, lives, fears and worry to God.

Previously, I talked about learning to submit to God's will, trusting that he knows our individual desires and needs. Learning to submit to God's will has many benefits for our lives. And one of these benefits is the freedom from worry.

When we rely solely on our own power and knowledge to direct our lives, it creates fear because we know, in the deepest part of ourselves, that there is much we do not see and understand. We know that we make mistakes because of our lack of knowledge. When we worry, we are continually trying to figure out what it is we are not seeing, or do not know. However, when we learn to give control of our lives to God and submit to his will, trusting his knowledge and care of us, it will remove fear and worry from our lives. It is impossible to truly trust God and submit to his will and still hang onto worry. It simply won't work.

When we choose to submit to God's will, we are relinquishing our power to make a choice or decision. We are choosing to allow God to make the choice and direct our actions. Therefore, there is nothing for us to do except that which God directs us to do. If we continue to be afraid, it is a statement of distrust of God's will for our lives, or that we have not truly submitted to God's will. If we continue to worry about finding a solution to a problem, we have not truly given the problem to God. When we worry about a problem that we have given to God, it is like telling God "I'm asking you to help me with this problem, but I'm going to try to figure it out for myself anyway". Now, I don't know about other people, but I find it kind of insulting when someone asks me for my help, then rejects my help by choosing to do what they know anyway. I wonder why they asked in the first place.

The way to eliminate worry, and the fear that causes it, is to give the problem to God. Yes, I believe that we are meant to use our minds and energies to make our choices and work to create our lives. However, our power and knowledge is limited. We need God's power and knowledge to assist us in creating the lives we desire. We need God's help to overcome our lack of knowledge and our fears.

Availing ourselves of God's assistance by submitting to His will eliminates fear and worry. When we choose to trust God for the answers and direction, there is no fear that the wrong choice will be made. When we trust God to know us, understand our needs and desires, and to use His power and knowledge for our happiness, there is absolutely nothing to fear. If there is nothing to fear, there is nothing to worry about.

The key to eliminate worry is in our relationship with God. Learn to trust God. Know that he knows who you are, what you need, what you desire, and that he wants, and is able, to supply all these things. When worry creeps in, take it to God. Through prayer, and remembering your trust in God, you will be able to put worry out of your life. You will be able to use your time and focus to appreciate and enjoy your life.

When you have done all you know to do, and have reached the limitations of your human capabilities, don't allow worry to rob you of your dreams, joy and happiness. Submit your will to God, trust Him to bring the knowledge, power, answers and directions to your life that you are lacking. Live each day with joy and happiness, knowing there is nothing to worry about when you have truly submitted your will to God.

CHAPTER 15
Fear

Fear is a very peculiar feeling. It can be a good thing, or detrimental to our lives. Fear can protect us from harm, or it can cripple our future. It all depends on what the fear is and how we handle it.

To understand fear, we must first understand what it is and how this came to be part of our emotions and perspectives. Fear, to be afraid, is an emotion caused by knowing there is the possibility of undesirable events taking place in our lives. It is our psychological way of trying to "brace for impact". Fear will cause us to absolutely avoid a situation if possible. If it is not possible to avoid a fearful situation, fear will cause us to try to mentally prepare for this event in order to attempt to minimize the pain, damage and/or disruption of our lives. Fear will cause us to ask ourselves "what if" over and over to try to mentally prepare ourselves to control what may happen.

One of the most beautiful things about youth is the lack of fear. We aren't born knowing fear, but learn it throughout our lives. It's necessary in our world to learn a certain amount of fear to protect our lives. We are taught to respect fire, steer clear of snakes, look both ways before crossing a road, etc. Although we hate to teach our children fear, we know that certain amounts of it are necessary to survival and health. However, too much fear can cripple your life. When a child becomes excessively fearful of pain or death, this extreme fear can rob the child of enjoying his life and experiences. Extreme fear can cripple the child's emotions and growth into adulthood. This kind of fear is not a good thing.

What we strive for as parents is to instill a proper balance of fear into a child's life. Don't be afraid to cross the road, just make sure there are no cars coming first. Fire is a good and useful tool, but you must respect it and use necessary precautions so you do not get burnt. Snakes are interesting creatures and belong to our world, but never forget they can hurt you. As in all things, balance is the key to the proper use of fear.

Yes, I did say the "use of fear". Fear does not have to be just an emotion that stops us from doing certain things. Fear can be used as a tool to help us make decisions for our lives and seek the knowledge and direction we need to pursue our desires. When we learn to use fear as a tool in our lives, we learn how to put it in proper balance.

To begin with, we need to be able to acknowledge our fear. There are certain areas of our lives that are easier to admit fear in (snakes) than other areas (a life change). Admitting to your fears is the first step in using them for a better future. Once you have acknowledged that you have this fear, you are then able to examine the details of the fear: what specifically you are afraid of, why you have this fear, is the fear valid, if the fear is valid can it be changed and if so, how. Once you learn the answers to these questions, you are then able to use this fear to guide you through it to achieve your desired results.

I want to use a couple of examples to help walk us through the steps of using fear as a tool to better our lives. Let's use the fear of snakes as an example. Say you have a big, beautiful yard that you love to spend time in, but you once saw a snake passing through and now you are afraid to go out and enjoy your lawn, even though you very much want to. So, we've done the first step, you don't go out to your lawn because you are afraid there may be a snake in it (this is acknowledging your fear as opposed to saying you just don't go out to the lawn because you don't want to). So now how do we turn this knowledge into a useful tool?

Let's answer the relevant questions: what specifically are you afraid of?—getting bitten by the snake. Why are you afraid of getting bitten by the snake—because you've been taught that they will bite you. Is this fear valid—yes, if I come across the snake it definitely could bite me. Can this situation be changed—yes. How—treat your property to repel snakes and learn what to do to protect yourself if you come across a snake. If you know that you have minimized the chance that you will have a snake on your property, and you have educated yourself to know how to protect yourself if you do see one, will this change your perspective about using your lawn? Yes.

We can learn to understand our fear and use this knowledge to guide us in the direction we need to take to accomplish our goals and desires.

For instance, say you have dreamed of learning to ski. Maybe you have said to yourself that you don't do it because you don't have the time or opportunity. Is the real reason because you are afraid to try it? If fear is the real reason holding you back, ask yourself the relevant questions. What specifically are you afraid of? Not having the skill to do this sport? The pain should you fall and injure yourself? Is your fear valid? Yes, you could fall and you may not be very good at it. Will not having the skill to be an Olympic skier mean that you shouldn't ski at all? Is it okay to do it just for fun whether you are good or not? If you get injured, are you reasonably certain that you will heal and be well again and that you will receive medical care to help you through the pain? Can this fear be changed? Yes, by starting out slow, with proper instruction, you will minimize the chance that you will be hurt. With proper instruction and practice you will acquire the skills to become better at the sport and increase your enjoyment.

By examining your fear, asking the questions that help you understand your fear, and using the answers to these questions to guide you to what you need to do to eliminate the fear, you will be able to expand your life and fulfill more of your desires. Fear need not be a stumbling block to your dreams and desires. If you learn to use fear as a tool, it can help you seek the ways and means to acquiring a fuller life.

I am not saying you need to eliminate every fear from your life. No, some of our fears protect us. But some of these fears are only a lack of knowledge that prevents us from fulfilling our hopes and dreams. Learning to examine and understand our fears will help us know when to keep a fear or when to use that fear as a tool to learn, grow and enhance our lives.

CHAPTER 16
Freewill, Fear and Faith

Humans are endowed with freewill. The ability to make their own choices in life. I've never met anyone that would dispute that. And we make these choices in hundreds of different ways each day. Even when we allow someone to make a choice for us, we still exercised our freewill in relinquishing our choice.

Our freewill is not just the actual choices we make, but includes the thoughts and beliefs we employ in making those choices. As we previously talked about, we can choose what we allow ourselves to think. Our thoughts are what form our belief systems. And it is our belief systems that guide our choices. If we allow other people to tell us what to think and believe, we are allowing other people to tell us how to use our freewill. However, what is right for one person's life is not necessarily right for anyone else. That is why it is so vital to know your own thoughts and beliefs and be the one choosing how to use your own freewill, not just allowing others to dictate your choices.

With all the information, opinions and viewpoints we are in contact with in any given day, knowing what to think or not think, believe and not believe, can be a murky problem. How does one sort out all this information and make a confident decision? The answer lies in knowing yourself. What makes you happy? What kind of person are you/do you want to be? What risks are you willing to take to pursue your happiness? What security do you need to feel happy?

Determining your own course in life, exercising our own freewill, is determined by the balance of fear and faith within you. Fear: expecting something bad or unpleasant to happen; as opposed to Faith: a firm belief/conviction in something for which there is no proof. Being able to make sound choices for ourselves is determined by how much we know about our own fears, faith and what balance is right for our own life.

Some of us are more open to risk and some of us are happier with more security. For example: some people like to skydive and other people don't even like to fly in planes. And there are those who like to fly, but not skydive. If you are a person whose happiness is increased by being able to skydive, it is up to you to use your freewill to make the choice. If you allow someone else to tell you that you should not skydive because they are afraid of it, you have relinquished your freewill to another person. You have also cheated yourself of an experience that would have enhanced your enjoyment of your life, based on someone else's fear. On the other hand, if you are not particularly interested in skydiving and do not feel it is an experience you would miss if you did not do it, why would you let someone influence you to take risks you don't want to take simply because they think you should experience it?

Before we can know what balance of fear and faith works for us, it is necessary to know what your own fears and faith are. It is very easy to adopt the fears or faith from other people's opinions and attitudes without realizing that we have not actually examined these thoughts and beliefs and determined their validity for ourselves. If you are afraid of something do you know why you are afraid of it? If you believe a certain choice in life will make you happy, do you know why you believe that? Is it because someone told you, or because you have examined the issue for yourself? Are you pursuing a career because you enjoy it and have dreamed of it, or because you have been influenced to believe it is the "right" thing to do? Have you not pursued a career you dreamed of because other people's opinions thought it is too risky or a waste of your life and talents? What do you think about it?

Sometimes the fear or faith we use in exercising our freewill has been adopted from the teachings and attitudes of those around us, but is not actually true to who we are as a person, or a conscious belief we have chosen. Examining these thoughts and beliefs, knowing what you believe as an individual and why you believe it, will allow you to use your freewill in a more purposeful manner in your life. As with any thoughts or thought processes, examine the fear or faith, determine which is true to you as an individual and discard that which is contrary to your belief system and who you are as a person. Instead of allowing your freewill to be influenced by someone else's belief system, you will be able to use your freewill to direct your life on a course that will be true to your own happiness.

In addition to choosing what fears and faith you adopt in your belief system, you also can choose the balance and use of these fears and faith. Fear will prevent or discourage you from a certain course of action; faith will encourage and lead you to a certain course of action. Both fear and faith are good, useful tools in choosing our paths in life, but also can be roadblocks to our happiness if we allow them to be out of balance.

Each choice we make for ourselves is an investment in our life. As with monetary investments, we invest based on our belief that we will receive a return that will enhance our lives. More money, more happiness, etc. Faith is what will allow us to make the investment (a firm belief that we will receive this return). Fear is what holds us back from investing (expectation of loss). The guide we use for investing in our lives is a balance between faith and fear. And just like we need to choose what we will fear or what we will have faith in, we need to choose for ourselves what balance of fear and faith is appropriate for our own freewill.

Some investors are comfortable with high risk investments. They understand the potential for loss and are confident in their ability to weather the loss and recover. Other investors are not as comfortable with loss, and therefore, choose to invest in a less risky manner. This is the same balance we can use to make our life choices. We need to know and understand, on an individual basis, what risks we are comfortable with taking and what security we need to feel. Other people cannot tell us what this balance should be. We need to examine our own dreams and goals for our own lives and decide for ourselves what risks we are willing to take or not, what balance of fear and faith will work in our happiness.

Sometimes we're the person who likes to fly, but not skydive. The return of seeing the world from such a high vantage point is exciting. But for some of us, seeing it from the plane is return enough compared to the risk of skydiving. And some people do not feel the need to see the world from that vantage point at all. It depends on who you are, and what works for your happiness.

Your freewill was given to you for directing your own life and happiness. How you choose to use it is entirely your decision. Your happiness in life will depend on knowing how to use your freewill in a purposeful manner, based on a balance of fear and faith as determined by you. You can let others decide what makes you happy, or you can use your freewill to make your happiness for yourself.

CHAPTER 17
Faith—It Requires Action

The term faith has several meanings. It can mean a strong belief, a religious belief, or trust in God and God's direction in our lives. The faith I want to talk about today is the trust we have in God and God's will and direction for our lives.

For many of us, our faith is our anchor in life. Faith provides us with the strength and determination to face life's difficult challenges. It is the strength of our faith that enables us to seek God's guidance and assistance in our lives.

But how do we know how strong our faith really is? How much do we really trust God to provide the guidance and support we need in our lives? The indication of the depth and strength of our faith is shown and known by our actions.

The King James Version of the Holy Bible, James 2:20-22 says: "(20) But wilt thou know, O vain man, that faith without works is dead? (21) Was not Abraham our father justified by works, when he had offered Isaac his son upon the altar? (22) Seest thou how faith wrought with his works, and by works was faith made perfect?" James was telling us here that it was Abraham's works that were the true indication of his faith. It is by our works, by our actions, that we truly declare our trust in God.

It is common to hear the statement: I have faith that God will make the way for me, or I have faith that God will give me the answer. And that's good. Owning your faith by acknowledging it, and claiming it, is a very good start. However, faith is not just in words and intentions. The true expression of faith is in the action. When God makes the way for you, are you willing to walk that way? When God gives you the answer, are you willing to accept it? It's easy to think that we will. But when the answer does not fall into our preconceived ideas of what God will do, or when the way shown to us is a path unknown, our willingness to trust is challenged.

The King James Version of the Bible, Isaiah 55:8 tells us: "For my thoughts are not your thoughts, neither are your ways my ways, saith the Lord." A clear-cut statement that God does not think, nor act, as we would think or act. That what we think the answers should be, or what we think God will do, is not necessarily the case. And this is when the true test of our faith occurs. Do we want God's direction and assistance enough to trust His ways and His thoughts? Are we willing to allow God to give us new information, something outside what we have previously known or believed?

When we think about it, what we know and believe is obviously not the answer, because we are asking for help, we are seeking new information and new ways. I have never read a definition of faith, nor heard an account of faith, that describes faith as "God answered my prayer the way I thought it should be done". No. Faith is trusting God for the solution and direction which we cannot find for ourselves. The strength of our faith is shown by our willingness to act upon the new information being given to us by God.

There are many accounts in the Bible where people have followed the direction of God in ways that were not only new to them, but contrary to their previously held beliefs. One such case is Judge Deborah who not only held a position not given to women at that time, but also helped lead an army for the deliverance of Israel. I can just imagine some of the criticism she must have suffered for having the faith to act upon God's direction, despite the popular belief of women's roles at that time. It would not have mattered how much Deborah prayed, or how much of the information from God she received. If Deborah had refused to act upon the new directions she received from God, the assistance and direction God gave her would have been meaningless. Deborah accomplished great things because she had the strength of faith to act upon God's direction.

So, the next time you find yourself stuck, praying, but not seeming to accomplish the change you are seeking, take a good, honest look at what is really happening. Have you received information you have rejected because it didn't seem to fit with your idea of the right solution? Has an opportunity presented itself, but you didn't take it because it was unfamiliar to you and you were afraid to try it? When new information and new opportunities did present themselves, and you were unsure of them because of your previously held beliefs, did you ask God to help you understand?

Real faith requires action. Not just the action of acceptance, but the action of doing. In addition to allowing ourselves to receive new information and direction, we also are required to put forth the effort to make the changes needed to accomplish what we are praying for. God will make opportunities, we are responsible for using our strength and abilities to use those opportunities.

Although God will carry us through times of hardships when we need His help, He will not carry us through life. We are given the power and strength to live our lives and we are expected to use it. And this applies to our faith also. God will give us answers. God will give us the information and direction we need to move forward in our lives. But it is up to us to have the faith to make that journey. It takes effort and determination to exercise trust. It is sometimes frightening to take the action our faith requires. This is when the true depth and strength of our faith will be known. When we are willing to walk through the fear, accept new paths and knowledge, and act upon the direction of God.

If you refuse to act when God is giving you answers, you may as well stop praying for help. It won't do you any good to get directions if you refuse to make the journey. However, if you truly have faith, trust God's direction in your life, you will act upon that direction. You will use the information and direction God gives you to make changes in your life.

This is faith: trusting God enough to take action with his direction and assistance.

Faith without action is meaningless. Faith with action will accomplish great things.

CHAPTER 18
Courage

Sometimes the things we learned to believe growing up are standing in the way of our happiness and fulfillment in life. Sometimes these beliefs are causing us to not be the person we want to be. Maybe it's a simple belief such as believing you do not have the talent to pursue a career you desire. Or maybe it's a major belief, like no longer believing in the religion you were raised in.

Do you sometimes question things that you have believed for most of your life? Do you sometimes feel a need or desire to change these beliefs because of new things you have learned, but are afraid to let go of traditions or expectations? Do you fear the rejection of family and community if you let these ideas and beliefs be known? I used to feel this way too. Until God showed me a new perspective about the story of Saul (the Apostle Paul) and the value of having the courage to change our lives.

Whether you are a Christian or not, believe in God or not, the story of the Apostle Paul still has meaning. If you are not familiar with the story, this is a brief summary:

The Apostle Paul's original name was Saul and he was from a place called Tarsus. Saul was both a Jew and a Roman citizen. But Saul did not accept Jesus of Nazareth as the Messiah and dedicated himself to the persecution of the followers of Jesus (Christians). Until he encountered the resurrected Jesus and began to believe that Jesus of Nazareth was the Messiah. Then he began to preach that Jesus was the Messiah and the Son of God. It is when he became one of Jesus' apostles that his name changed from Saul to Apostle Paul.

My point in discussing this incident is not about whether Jesus is the Messiah/Son of God or not. The point that I want to talk about here is Paul's life change; what it meant for him on a personal level.

We all grow up having adopted belief systems from the influences around us: family, friends, schools, religions, television and so on. But these belief systems often change over time. We learn new information, become more aware of our own perspectives and adapt our beliefs to this new knowledge.

Changing your belief system inside of yourself is one thing. Changing your life in response to the change in your belief system is quite another. As much as our world was created to change, humans still resist change. We have seen this phenomenon played out time and time again in history. People who become aware that they don't believe in the religion of their family but adhere to it anyway so as not to be ostracized from the family, people who are not particularly interested in or suited for a certain career but pursue it anyway because of familial tradition, etc. We stay in these belief systems and life situations because it is far more comfortable and secure than changing our lives. But sometimes, for some people, the change is imperative.

It was for Saul. Saul could not deny his changed perspective and what it meant for his life. Until his encounter with Jesus, Saul was famous for his role as one of the most fierce and dedicated persecutors of Christians, feared by many people. He had a very strong belief that to follow Jesus (be a Christian) was heresy and this following needed to be stopped. And for good reason. The whole story surrounding Jesus: his parents, his birth, his lowly life and especially the new and formerly unheard-of ideas he preached were all contrary to everything Saul was raised to believe and lived his whole life.

And then he met the resurrected Jesus. The new knowledge, what he learned about Jesus, changed his perspectives and consequently his beliefs. So, what to do? How could he possibly continue to persecute and imprison people for what he, himself now believed to be true?

So, okay, he obviously would need to stop persecuting the followers of Jesus. But what about his reputation? How was he going to deal with what everyone knew and thought about him? If Saul was like a lot of people, he would simply have made his excuses: tired of the work, too old to do this anymore, have other things I need to do, etc. Then just quietly fade into the background, find another line of work, and would not make his change of heart so apparent.

But Saul didn't do this. Oh, no. Not only did he not hide his change in perspectives and beliefs, but he became just as famous for being a follower of Jesus as he was for being a persecutor of Jesus' followers. Can you imagine how difficult this transition was for Saul? How much courage and dedication it took for him to become the Apostle Paul? When we read the account, we think about the glory and position the Apostle Paul had as one of Jesus' most trusted and revered apostles. But what about what it took for him to get there?

It's relatively easy to understand that he was ridiculed and persecuted by the people who still fought against Christianity. That's to be expected. And it's even understandable that he would be persecuted even more for his following Jesus, since he was formerly a persecutor. But can you imagine what it cost him with regard to his standing in his community? His job, his family and friends; his credibility as a person? These aspects of his changing beliefs and life alone would be extremely difficult to bear. He could no longer lead the life he had lived and would not be accepted in the community he belonged to. But he also would not be readily accepted into the community and life of those who followed Jesus. Just because Saul now believed in Jesus as the Messiah, and began to follow his teachings, does not mean that he was accepted by the Christian community. They feared him. This would have been an extremely lonely road for Saul to walk. Even being befriended by Jesus and others following him would not take the pain and insecurity out of such a major upheaval of the life he had always known.

However, there is the possibility that there was an even greater obstacle to this great change in Saul's life. The self-doubt created by the disbelief that anyone would ever put value on what he had to say because of what he used to be. Since I have never had an opportunity to speak to Saul/Apostle Paul to know exactly what he felt, I will not presume to say that he did feel this way. But as a person, and knowing how other people might feel in such circumstances, I can't help but wonder just how difficult it was for Saul to have the courage to begin preaching and promoting the very person and beliefs he so adamantly warred against.

When I imagine myself in the same circumstances, I find the task almost impossible. Because you know you are despised and rejected by most of the people you are trying to join, and you are equally despised and rejected by most of the people whose beliefs you are leaving. Who's going to listen to you? You'll be a laughingstock. And for what? No one will believe what you have to say anyway.

So, what would make a person like Saul have the courage and dedication not only to change his beliefs and his life, but to walk the difficult path of encouraging and helping others to change their beliefs and lives too? The understanding that your life, and the lives of others, is worth the courage it takes to change. Knowing that having the courage to change your life will make you a better person, with a better life.

When Saul received new information that changed his beliefs, he had the courage to change his life. When Saul recognized the good brought about in his life by this change, he had the courage and dedication to bring this information to others, so their lives could benefit from it. Saul refused to be self-indulgent and selfish by refusing to overcome the difficulties created in his life by embracing change, refusing to suffer the objection and rejection from others, and denying his ability to give this information to others.

Saul's life wasn't just about meeting Jesus and becoming a believer in Christianity. Saul's life was an example of having the courage to change, and to do what we are inspired to do for the good of all humanity. Don't allow what happened yesterday, what you used to be, what you used to believe, to stop you from being what you are meant to be. Have the courage to learn new perspectives, accept changes in your belief system and change your life accordingly. Have the courage to be the person you want to be and help others to do the same.

CHAPTER 19
Giving—It Keeps Us Connected

We all know that charitable giving—our time, work, money, attention, care and support—helps us feel good about who we are as a person and helps create bonds with other people. Charitable giving is encouraged in the Bible and is the basis of the "Pay It Forward" concept. Giving is a good thing to do.

Giving also promotes the cohesion of humanity. When we give of ourselves to others, we are acknowledging and renewing our connection to other people. This is an extremely vital element of our lives. In our modern times, humanity has become self-absorbed and centered around individual interests. Because of these viewpoints and life choices, we have lost much of our human connections and the feeling of belonging to a community. Many people struggle with loneliness. Loneliness is a result of losing our connections to other human beings. We all need and want to be connected to other people, to feel we are a part of humanity.

To feel connected to other people, we need to acknowledge their needs as humans on the same level as our own. This requires time, attention and opportunity. Giving to others provides this opportunity. When we give to others, we are taking the time and attention to become aware of their need and to accept responsibility for supplying this need. The action of giving will acknowledge both the giver and receiver as a valued person.

These acts do not need to be great or big things. Sometimes just a simple act of kindness will provide a feeling of connectedness to other people, and possibly the opportunity to develop a new friendship. In our daily lives, we are so busy focusing on our "to do" list, and lack of time to accomplish all we want to accomplish, that we selfishly push through our days unaware of the needs and burdens of those around us. Learning to become aware of those around us and their needs, and acting upon that awareness to give to others, will provide us with the feeling of being connected to and being a part of humanity.

Something as simple as allowing a mother with a couple of toddlers to go ahead of us in the grocery line will acknowledge her burden and your willingness to give of your time in support and care for her and her children. Yielding to someone in traffic even though you have the right-of-way is an acknowledgement of their needs. Yes, you are busy. But so are other people. Acknowledging another person's busy day, and allowing those extra seconds or minutes for them, will be much more valuable than the time sacrificed to do so. Not only will you feel better about the person you are, but you will have promoted the connection between people. You will have acknowledged the connection you share as human beings. These examples may not allow the time and chance for creating new friendships, but they will create a sense of belonging and connection between ourselves and those around us.

When we give to others it also helps us understand how to be a good recipient. Being a good recipient of charitable acts is as important as being a good giver. It takes two for the process to work. Many times, when we are offered assistance or unexpected kindnesses, we feel unentitled to receive what is offered, either because we feel we should not take from others, or because we feel it should go to someone who needs it more than we do. However, if you have experienced the joy of the human connections created by giving, you will understand that receiving what is offered is as important to the giver as it is to the receiver. We need to connect to one another through these acts of kindness and assistance. These are the things that keep us connected to each other, aware of the importance of each other's lives and the humanity we all share.

Try to practice giving something of yourself to the world each day. Give a smile, a helping hand, a compliment, the time to listen. Each time you make the effort to give something to someone else, you renew your connection to other people. Each time you renew your connection to other people, you make your life stronger, happier and healthier.

CHAPTER 20
Boundaries

Boundaries are something we live with every day. Boundaries serve practical purposes for our lives. The fence that borders our yards to keep our pets and children in a safe area. The social boundaries we use as guidelines to protect the interests and dignity of individuals in public. The markings on a ball field that enable the players to follow the rules of the game. Boundaries are a good and useful tool.

Knowing and exercising your boundaries as an individual is necessary for a productive and healthy life. Personal boundaries are what we use to feel secure in our world as a person, and to define to the world what actions and behaviors are acceptable, or not, regarding our person. Not having clearly defined boundaries, and/or not protecting the boundaries you do have, can cause problems and dysfunction in your life. We need to define for ourselves, as adults, the choices and limitations we will set for our own actions as well as the limitations of allowable actions from the world around us.

As part of growing up we learn to form boundaries according to our personalities. This is a natural part of becoming an adult. We learn who we are as individuals and learn how to make choices per our likes and dislikes. This will naturally cause us to form boundaries for our lives, both physical and internal. However, there are many things that influence how we form our boundaries and how we maintain our boundaries. As we become adults, our boundaries are influenced by the opinions and teachings of others. Some of these will be acceptable to our adult person, but others will hinder our ability to function according to our own needs and beliefs.

Have you ever been in a situation where someone asked something of you and on the inside you were thinking "no, I don't really want to do this", but on the outside you said "yes, I'll be happy to"? Did you agree to do this thing because you felt obligated to be "nice" and do this thing whether you wanted to or not. This is the kind of influence I am referring to when I talk about other people's opinions influencing our boundaries. What you have been taught has overridden your personally chosen limits.

I am not saying that every time we do something we'd rather not is a violation of our boundaries. Our relationships need compromise and flexibility in our boundaries to a certain degree. What I am talking about here are the boundaries that define our lives. The boundaries that help us to be and become what we desire for ourselves.

Continually allowing the opinions and teachings of others to influence our boundaries is detrimental to our success in life. Being a nice person is one thing, feeling obligated to sacrifice your needs and wants for those of others will ruin your ability to accomplish your dreams and happiness. So how then do we balance our boundaries with our need for compromise in our relationships?

It starts with self-honesty. When we are confronted with a request that is contrary to what we want for ourselves, we need to be able to take the time to examine the request, compare it to what we want and decide what is most important to our own goals and happiness. Although this may sound terribly selfish, it is not. We cannot make successful, happy relationships if we are not happy. Continually putting someone else's happiness ahead of our own will cause us not to be happy within the relationship. And compromise is not a one-sided action. Compromise should include your happiness as well as that of the other person.

So, when we are considering giving the other person what they are requesting, we need to be honest about our own happiness. If sacrificing our own needs and desires for that of the other person will make us unhappy, or inhibit our goals and dreams, here is a boundary we need to define for ourselves. And not only define for ourselves, but maintain by not allowing ourselves to feel obligated to do things that are contrary to our goals and happiness.

Other such boundaries include the way people speak to us, our financial resources, respect of our privacy and so on. Knowing who we are as a person and maintaining the boundaries that define this person allows us to become and accomplish our future according to our dreams for happiness. Allowing others to violate our boundaries, continually giving over to others that which we need to maintain for ourselves, will only defeat our attempts to create the life we dream of.

Another aspect of boundaries that can defeat our life's goals and plans are the boundaries we have created throughout our lives that are no longer necessary or useful, but still influence our lives. Throughout our lives things happen that cause us pain or fear. When things like this happen, we often develop a boundary or wall that helps to protect us and cope with the pain and fear. This usually starts in our childhood, when we are incapable of understanding a different way to deal with these occurrences.

For instance, as a child you may have suffered the loss of a grandparent that you were close to. This may have caused you to fear losing someone you have become close to in the future. Consequently, you may have created a boundary against getting close to other people. At the time you developed this boundary, it helped you deal with your grief by making you feel a bit safer. However, in your adult life, this same boundary could prevent you from making the close relationships you desire. An examination of this boundary, and making the efforts to change or eliminate it, will open the way for you to accomplish the relationships you desire.

There are many ways that we may have created boundaries in our past that are effecting our future. The things we are taught by others: teachers, religious leaders, television, politicians and even our families, may be contrary to our own beliefs and have created boundaries we have not been aware of. Boundaries that have stood as roadblocks in our paths to accomplish our dreams and hopes for our lives. Sometimes these boundaries have been created by our own perceptions at a particular time in our lives, perceptions that no longer hold true. What is needed here is an honest examination of these boundaries and their effect or usefulness in our future.

When we are struggling with an aspect of our lives we want to change, but seem to be unable to change, we need to look at the boundaries we have that interfere with our goals.

Going back to our previous example: imagine that you have an elderly neighbor that you find interesting and would like to get to know better. But something keeps stopping you. If you examine your boundaries, you may find that the wall you put up when you lost your grandparent is now stopping you from getting to know your neighbor. Realizing as an adult that you are now able to cope with loss, in a way you were not equipped to as a child, will enable you to relinquish the walls you no longer need. Being able to remove this wall, by realizing that it is no longer necessary, will open the way for you to make the friendship with your neighbor you desire.

It is necessary to be aware of the boundaries in our lives. We need to know what is a useful, goal maintaining boundary or what boundaries are detrimental to our lives. We need to actively maintain the boundaries that promote our goals and happiness, and eliminate those boundaries that are preventing us from achieving our goals and happiness. A happy, healthy life is created by maintaining the boundaries that promote your future goals and desires, and only the boundaries that promote your future goals and desires.

CHAPTER 21
Gratitude Is Healthy

As a giver of good deeds or gifts, it is rewarding to have your thoughts and efforts on someone else's behalf recognized and appreciated. Having someone express their gratitude to you for something you did for them makes you feel good about yourself and happy for choosing to give to another person. Gratitude from someone is confirmation that our gift has been accepted and appreciated. However, gratitude is just as important to the receiver of good gifts as it is to the giver. The expression of gratitude creates thought patterns and habits of a healthy mind.

The more we focus on the good things in our lives, and eliminate the negative thoughts, the happier we are. The expression of gratitude is a habit that helps keep our focus on the positive side of our lives. When we practice expressing gratitude every day, throughout our day, we will find it almost impossible to think negative thoughts. For example: someone cuts you off in traffic and has caused you to have to slam on your brakes to avoid an accident. Instead of being angry at the other driver (maybe they do deserve it, but your anger won't change anything) choose to be grateful for your good brakes that enabled you to avoid damage to your car and your person. Mentally or verbally express that gratitude. If your focus is on the good and positive part of the event (having good brakes) you will feel joy instead of anger.

When we express gratitude, either in thought or by word, we are reaffirming the good things in our lives. By choosing to focus on the positive aspects of our lives, being grateful for what we have and what we receive, we do not allow negative attitudes to rob us of our happiness and joy. The expression of gratitude helps us maintain our focus on what is good and right in our lives.

The expression of gratitude will promote feeling more secure in our lives. The expression of gratitude is not only an acknowledgement of a gift, but also the acknowledgement of being loved and cared for. Whether we have received a blessing from God or another person, acknowledging this gift with gratitude reminds us that we are loved and cared for, which increases our feeling of security.

When we acknowledge being loved and cared for, it also generates an awareness of our relationship to the giver. Being consciously aware, through expressed gratitude, that we have received an expression of love and care will strengthen the bond and relationship we have with the giver. The expression of gratitude tells the giver that their love and care is wanted, accepted and appreciated.

Having gratitude for the blessings we receive in life is not just about what we owe to God and other people for their help to us. Expressing our gratitude is also about focusing on the good and positive aspects of our lives, increasing our feelings of security through acknowledging that we are loved and cared for, and allowing the opportunities to build stronger relationships with God and those who show us love and care. Gratitude is not an obligation, but an opportunity. Every time we express gratitude, in thought or word, we are availing ourselves of the opportunity to be more positive, feel more secure and to build stronger relationships.

Gratitude is good for those who are receiving it, and good for those who are giving it. Having and expressing gratitude is a habit of a healthy life.

CHAPTER 22
Courage or Irresponsible Choices

Courage. It is the substance of heroes, the backbone of change, the celebrated characteristic of leaders. Courage is associated with intelligence and strength. Courage is what has enabled our world to make the changes needed to advance and improve. Unfortunately, courage is seldom recognized for what it is until after it is proven. Most often the person exercising courage is considered foolhardy and irresponsible until achieving success in their actions, or the action is judged as a worthy sacrifice for good. Only after accomplishing a great deed, or an attempt at a great deed, are these actions then translated as courage. Why is this?

The answer to this question lies in our perceptions of the lives and choices of other people. Each person is both physical and spiritual. We have an "outside" life and an "inside" life. It is easy for us to view the outside life of other people and make judgments about their choices and actions, based upon our own understanding. What we cannot see is the inside life of other people. We cannot fully know the needs, desires, hopes and dreams that live within another individual. Therefore, we cannot know what the driving force behind their choices and actions truly is.

Even when we are close enough to other individuals to be confided in, and allowed to know some of their internal life, we can never truly know the whole of the person. We are unable to truly comprehend the need for change within them, or the strength and determination it will take for them to accomplish this change. We are then left with only our own perspective, based upon what we see and comprehend from our own internal world. And often the choices and actions taken by other people look crazy, foolish and sometimes irresponsible to us. Many times, we cannot see the courage of an action or choice until it is accomplished. Because we cannot not see the need and drive within another person for changes in their life, we cannot understand their need to risk loss, or jeopardize part of their life, to grow and improve their world.

Knowing this will help us become more tolerant and less critical of the changes other people seek to make in their lives. Just because their choices and actions look crazy or irresponsible to us does not make it true. We simply don't know what is behind their decision.

What does make the difference between irresponsible choices and courage? Responsibility. Taking responsibility for the outcome of our choice and not expecting other people to bail us out of the consequences of our choices.

Change inevitably requires some degree of sacrifice. If we want to change our career, we will need to sacrifice the security and seniority of our current position. If we want to change where we live, we will need to sacrifice our proximity to friends or family we currently live near and the comfort of familiar surroundings. It takes courage to give up the comfortable, secure and familiar for the uncomfortable, uncertain and strange. When we are willing to take responsibility for these sacrifices, whether we accomplish our desired goal or not, it is courageous. It takes courage to take a risk knowing that you will lose some of your comfort and security.

It's when we make choices for change but expect other people to sacrifice for those choices that we practice irresponsible choices. It is not courage if you expect other people to make the sacrifices to replace or provide what you lose. It is not courage if you expect other people to provide a "safe net" so you will not lose the things you don't want to sacrifice. It is irresponsible to expect other people to sacrifice for your desires and goals.

So, what does this mean for our lives? Two things.

One: if we want change in our lives we must be willing and able to make the sacrifices needed to make the change. To have the courage to move forward in your life, you must be responsible for the decisions and choices these changes require. It is irresponsible to expect other people to make the sacrifices for your desires and goals.

Two: When we make choices in our lives, inevitably there will be those people who will tell us that we are being irresponsible. That choosing to make sacrifices or risk certain areas of our lives for changes we desire is irresponsible. But only you can make that determination for your life. Are you able to take responsibility for the choices you make? Do you expect to take responsibility for potential losses you may suffer? What may be irresponsible for someone else may be courage for you.

Sometimes it is difficult to make choices and changes in our lives when we are being criticized by the people around us because they are unable to know what our needs and desires are and why we need these changes. Sometimes we can feel like we are being irresponsible for taking risks and making changes that other people think we should not do. But look insides yourself. How important is this change to you? Are you willing to be responsible for the risks you are taking? Will you have the courage to suffer the sacrifice and be responsible for the outcome? Only you can know whether your choices are irresponsible or courage. How other people judge these choices in the end will depend on your level of responsibility. It will be your actions that will determine if you are being courageous or irresponsible.

Conclusion

When I look back over my life, I am amazed not only at what I have experienced and learned, but also the ways I have taken control of the person that I am.

When I was growing up, I used to hear people say: "well, that's just the way I am". I understood this phrase to mean that we are the way we are and there is nothing we can do about that. I'm very, very happy to know that there is something I can do about that. I can change me. I can choose not only what career I want to work, where I want to live, etc., but I can choose to be the person I want to be.

It is my perspective that the truest form of freedom is the freedom to be the person I want to be. And I now know that the only person who can take that freedom from me is me.

Learning that I am in control of what I believe, what I think and what I will accept for my person is the greatest knowledge I have acquired. I hope that it will be for you, too.

Nancy

Printed in the United States
By Bookmasters